To my family for their love and support. To my friends for their love and support.

Thank you to Dr. George and Martha Robertson for their support and encouragement. To Dr. Robertson, thank you for time and proofing of this special project.

To myself, continue to believe in Jesus, put God first and trust in the guidance of the Holy Spirit.

Preface

Throughout the years I have started and stopped towards publishing my first book. Although my poetry, psalms, essays, and meditations have been published in other formats, publishing this book was more intimate for me. One humble preface by E.E. Cummings says that "the poems to come are for you and for me and not for most people." The writings to come "are for me and for you and not for most".

"I will meditate also of all thy work and talk of thy doings" Psalms 77:12 KJV.

I wanted to provide an unorthodox contemplation of life's experiences, through scriptural reference and reflection, sharing in a small space, a glimpse of intimacy with God.

Contents

Conversations & Prayers

Girls and their fathers

Do girls need their dad?

That is a two-edged sword when that question is posed. I can only answer it from my perspective.

I recall being nineteen years old, and I had just moved off campus during my sophomore year in college. I grew up knowing who my mother said my father was. I remember him coming around when I was about eight years old, and I also remember him being in federal prison. He was serving a ten-year sentence down in Miami. I recall receiving a phone call from him when I was about eighteen years old because I would always track the timeline from my memory at eight and the length of sentence. He had just gotten out of jail.

The conversation was brief, very brief. I do remember telling him that I was in college now. Fast forward several years, I am now thirty-two years old, and another man shows up, claiming to be my dad. I knew who he was, I knew of him, but I never knew that he believed he was my dad until that time. At thirty-two years old, I was not interested in knowing either way. During this time, I was a working and productive citizen. I had bought my first house, about to sell the same house and was heading towards working on my doctorate degree. I was not interested in knowing, "who was the father".

So, when the question is posed about children and their dad, I say it's a two-edged sword because I can only answer from my perspective. On one hand, at nineteen years old, off campus, in a city without any family, I recall crying because he wasn't there. I recall crying because I

felt like if he had only known what I had been through and was going through, that maybe things would have been different. Now understand that my relationship with my mother didn't get "good" until 2010. She was not someone I could call on when I needed to and if I needed to or if I needed to. I was out here making it by myself. At nineteen years old I was working full-time and overtime, in college full-time, and navigating this thing called life with difficulty. Much difficulty. Many mistakes.

I had finished high school at seventeen years old, graduating Licensed Practical Nursing (LPN) school at the same time and was now in a city, in a strange land, alone. Again, crying out at that age, longing for a dad, for a father, just someone else to support me, lift me up when I couldn't myself. God had other plans. I speak to other young people, woman, or man, that if you're growing up

without a dad, don't let society's expectations limit God's direction.

It is not always ripe for you to understand his direction but to trust that he has his hands on you. For me, not having a dad, did not deter anything that was planned for my life. Sure, it was most definitely difficult. Sure, he has and had other kids. Sure, the second man, who said he was my dad, had a whole family. However, the supposed proclamations to my paternal heritage, did not include me. I finished high school, went from being a seventeen-year-old LPN to having a doctorate degree in nursing at thirty-four years old. I speak to my own daughter, who grew up knowing who her biological dad is, because I was married at the time, but me being a single parent for fourteen years.

It is because of my own experiences and story that I made sure she knew of him but when she became of age, we had to have the "talk". And, that talk is for another life chapter, not this one. I am currently remarried and have a wonderful husband who is also an even better dad to my daughter. My daughter understands that she has never lacked, she has never wanted and if she ever gets to a position of crying out, she will know of different father. A heavenly father. One who is able to abide with you, if you abide him. One who is able to lead when you lack understanding and guide when lack direction. He is a father, to the fatherless and a mother to the motherless.

"A father of the fatherless, and a judge of the widows, is God in his holy habitation."
Psalms 68:5 KJV

Longsuffering

Early on, I never knew what I could take until I was placed into a situation. Being pushed to your wits end, the towel is damp and too heavy to throw in, you learn the concept of bearing your cross. Battles come with very few options and giving up not being one of them.
I had to experience life's undeserving circumstances to value the power of forgiveness.

Eight. Eight years old. I knew at eight years old that I did not want to grow up and become like those around me. The only option I had was school. I knew that I must go to school, finish, and go to college to leave. I was the first in my family to finish high school. The first in my family to go to college, and finish.

I am so grateful to the schoolteachers and parents of friends who were blessings to me.

It was the determination to leave that compelled me towards my career in nursing. Nursing chose me, I did not choose it. My plan during high school was to become a neurosurgeon or psychiatrist. I had been a pre-med magnet student since middle school. I was going to be a doctor. Life happened and that first desire was put on the backburner. I am a college student majoring in nursing, working as an LPN and I was just trying to survive. I was working evening shift this particular day and the nurse working the shift with me, walked by me, tapped me on my back and spoke- "that doctor that you want to be, you're going to be". No truer words were spoken.

"So shall my word be that goeth forth out of my mouth: it shall not return unto me void, but it shall accomplish that which I please, and it shall prosper in the thing whereto I sent it." Isaiah 55:11

Along the journey towards achieving this doctorate there was failure, doubt, and never starting at all. God knows what his plans for your life are. He knows how he intends to use those plans to accomplish his purposes in this earth. The desires that are placed in your heart, he placed them there. He tends the garden. He sends some to plant, water, prune, and he is the master of increase. He gives the increase. Your plans may not be aligning with what your desires are but if you just stay the course. His words will accomplish what it was set in motion to do.

Untold Story

There is a story, that I don't talk about as often as I probably should. It doesn't usually come up in random conversations and it isn't one that I necessarily perseverate on. It was summer break of that transitional period from the freshman year to the sophomore year. I had already had years pf battling suicidal ideations, but no one knew about them.

Obviously, I had unsuccessful attempts at suicide while growing up. That may be another story I'll share later but if I may interject, parents check on your kids. This time was the last time, and it was different. I had a nervous breakdown. I had spent an entire day, crying and I couldn't stop crying. I was in my campus apartment, and I had a

remaining bottle of nineteen Tylenol gel capsules. I took them all. I went to work the next day still feeling weighed down and emotionally numb.

Long story short, I ended up in the emergency room of a local hospital. I told the physician what I had done before coming to work and she looked at me strange. She told me that I should be dead given the amount of Tylenol I had taken. Tests were completed and more people came in to speak with me. I was admitted to a psychiatric unit under the Baker-Act.

I went through the process of admittance. I met young person while I was there.. He was about the age that I was, said that he wanted to be a lawyer, but he did something that I so uniquely remember. He took me on a personal tour of the facility, and he pointed to every picture

that was hanging on the wall. As he pointed to the pictures, he explained how everything related back to God. We would get to a picture of a fish, and he told me about Jesus. Before I left the facility, I went through some counseling and my mother came up so that I could be released; however, this same young man wrote me a poem. The poem, I still have. It wasn't until years later that I realized what had happened.

We can be in some of the darkest of places, places of desperation and the Lord will seek you out. You can turn to the left, turn to the right, or keep running all together. You can be in the desert where there isn't a visible road to lead to anywhere, and you will run into God. At a time when I wanted to end it all and tried, he was with me. I was on the brink of what should have been death, where death was following me, but the Lord provided comfort and deliverance.

I realize that life in of itself, is the purpose and plan. It is the

Lord's purpose that we are here to help one another and his

plan that live under the banner of his grace.

"Yea, though I walk through the valley of the shadow of death, I will fear no evil: for thou art with me; thy rod and thy staff they comfort me." Psalm 23:4

Who are you?

For a long time, I never exactly knew how to answer that question. Riddled with childhood trauma, misdirected responsibilities, and buried dreams, I did not who I was. Growing up in South Florida is and was exactly what is now for most of us who grew up there. When I say South Florida, I mean Fort Lauderdale. We moved around a lot because we were on government assistance, and no one place, or city was just home.

The first lesson into the knowledge of who you are, starts at home. Home was a place of traumatic memories. If it were not for the undue parental name calling, I might have known and believed in who I was sooner.

The maternal rants of being called everything that I wasn't. To my schoolteachers and schoolmates, I was smart, talented, a friend, a poetry writer. I was Katoria. My molestation started when I was about seven years old and when I told it, I wasn't believed. When my grandmother and godmother asked me, "who has been bothering you". I told who it was. Like most adults, it was pushed under the rug, and I was pushed into silence.

There is a family who lived next door to my godmother. I don't know if they assumed or knew but every summer, they took me in to spend with their kids, they were saving me from molestation. This family took me to church on Saturdays. I went to Naples on their family trips. I spent Sabbath in their living room singing hymns, fasting, and praying. They laid a foundation that is woven into my story of God's plan.

I had to tell the story again at fifteen years old. I remember the day. Juanita Bynum was getting big with her preaching, and I was sitting in the living room. My mom was there, her best friend was there. I was sitting there, watching one of her sermons and I was moved to tears. She was preaching her *"No more sheets"* message [1997]. I was crying uncontrollably. I was asked, what's wrong. It was then I recounted what happened to me as a child. My mother responded, she knew but because her lifestyle choices at the time, there wasn't anything she could do. No one understood the repeated visual images that I carried, that would play out in my head like movie reels. No one knew that while I would sit alone in my room, listening to music and writing, that I would be alone in the house crying and praying. I didn't even understand the significance of lonely moments in my room.

I didn't understand that I was praying. It would still take me several years to speak about the story to others, from a position of power and not shame. But a new day came.

"Before I formed thee in the belly I knew thee; and before thou camest forth out of the womb I sanctified thee, and I ordained thee a prophet unto the nations."
Jeremiah 1:5 KJV.

I was around twenty or twenty-one years old. It was a Friday morning. I was at work, working dayshift. I had an overwhelming sense to pray; about nothing in particular, but to pray. The feeling was so heavy that I kneeled at the medication cart and pretended as though I was looking for something in the bottom drawer and bowed my head. I was praying. It was as though that didn't satisfy the tugging.

I proceeded to go into a bathroom and run the water as though I was washing my hands, and I prayed. The feeling would not leave me. I left work that Friday and by that Sunday morning, I was in church. I was in church, wearing a teal-colored button-down shirt, black skirt and stockings, black shoes. I stood in the pew row and was afraid to move for the altar call, but I reminded myself of that Friday. I went to the altar. The pastor of the church was doing what God sent him to do, and I stood there. He already been by me, put some oil on me, and moved on.

Something, and we know what the something, wanted to convince me to go back to my seat, nothing was wrong with me and that I would be alright. My feet would not move. The pastor came back over to me and whispered in my ear, "out of your mother's womb you were chosen".

The rest of what he said, I could not tell you because that was all I remembered hearing. I heard the stories of those who were in attendance of what happened while I was at the altar. I know the story of the transformation that happened after I got up. After, I got up in Jesus' name. So, who am I? What I am not, is defeated. I am not what the critics, the demographics, or the naysayers say I am. I am saved. I am delivered. I am a daughter of God. I am sinner who was made whole and set free. The traumas of my youth no longer hold me in bondage. I am a teacher. I am an evangelist. I am who God says I am.

"For I know the plans I have for you, declares the LORD, plans for welfare and not for evil, to give you a future and a hope. Then you will call upon me and come and pray to me, and I will hear you."
Jeremiah 29:11-12

Meditations

It is in these moments of reflection that I write. I write

poetry, psalms, and the meditations of my heart. A

poetical timeline of God's redemptive power. A timeline to

chronicle the deliverance of God's love. A memorial

landmark of what God has been to me and in my life. I

pray that these writings provide a beacon of hope where

you may find your way towards his everlasting peace.

"Moreover I will make a covenant of peace with them; it shall be an everlasting covenant with them" Ezekiel 37:26

Trials

There are some things that happen to us in life, that we didn't ask for nor did we do anything to cause it. Events happen and often come to cripple us, but God uses it to shape us. Incidents are going to make you feel like quitting, but you must remember what you must do. Unless someone else has experienced it, no one can ever understand why it happened to you and not them. We are not born with targets on our foreheads and there is no way to explain how the cards are dealt.

Sometimes we grow weary, and inpatient, often forgoing our best intentions. We overlook the obvious, turn a deaf ear to that still small voice, and proceed on our own accord. If we can remember in our carnal haste to be patient, and faint not, we shall inherit that which is due.

Much like the seed that grows on the side of a cliff, the storms, rain, and winds abound, but deep within there is growth and strength taking root. So, it is for us. As it is written in *Matthew 6:28 KJV, "see how the Lilies of the field grow".* Take heart in knowing that He is taking care of what is promised. If you know the cliché', *don't put the cart before the horse*, then the word for today is, **don't put the promise before the manifestation**.

All things fall into place in its own time. Things that once seemed down, will be up. All impossible ideas and dreams will become manifested. Life has a way of deleting the past and depositing it into the future. He takes situations and circumstances that once was bad and make it a different picture. God has his way of orchestrating and organizing little coincidences into a planned destiny. It is by our doubts that we fail.

We fail to see as God sees and fail to believe as hope and faith mandates. It is in our lack of confidence and trust that we cannot see how a dead situation will become a walking and breathing Lazarus.

Contrary to what one may think, it is not that we lack the patience of Job, but more so we merely lack the courage of Joshua when God told him that he would lead the people into the promise land. We so often lack the diligence of Elijah when he prayed and prayed for the rain to return. Or we lack the perseverance of Joseph to endure while God fulfills his promise. Maybe we're like Jonah, lacking repentance and refusing to give way to God's plan and the path set before us. Do we deny the spirit of change because of fear or intimidation? Are there are items on the shelf or in storage, or views from unopened doors that we do not, see?

Perhaps because of scientific explanations of time and space, that our flesh is forced to rush or disregard the complexities of consequential events. If we would but pause, to see past what is set before us, perhaps then we can see what is beyond us.

I want to encourage you that in time you will find what has been hidden. In time, you will embrace what is planted on the inside of you. Your time in this world will not end until you have accomplished all that God has designed for you. Time changes all things for the good and that God is working through all things for your good!

Timing

I have observed something else under the sun. The fastest runner doesn't always win the race, and the strongest warrior doesn't always win the battle. The wise sometimes go hungry, and the skillful are not necessarily wealthy. And those who are educated don't always lead successful lives. It is all decided by chance, by being in the right place at the right time.

"I returned, and saw under the sun, that the race is not to the swift, nor the battle to the strong, neither yet bread to the wise, nor yet riches to men of understanding, nor yet favour to men of skill; but time and chance happeneth to them all." Ecclesiastes 9:11KJV

Here lies the secret of the will of God for our purpose and what should fuel our determination. It is not by our skillful intent and the attaining of degrees that we have succeeded, became wealthy, or completed a task before our constituents. The very thing that has propelled the rags to riches, the idiot to savant, is the fervent fire that has ignited untouched passion.

Many philosophers and celebrities proclaim their discovery of such and such secrets or tapping into wealth. The Hebrew definition for the word chance is "unforeseen meeting or event, fate". But herein scripture has the very mystery of the influence of God's strength on our lives and his plans for our destiny. Ecclesiastes points not to the luck, as is seen with gambling, but it points to the choice that is determined by being in line with God's Word.

When we are in line with God's Word for our life,

then we have positioned ourselves in the right place at the

right time where God's plan is able to unfold. The almighty

redeemer, the creator who has formed the sun has also

orchestrated unforeseen events to take place in our lives.

The blueprint is in plain view on heaven's table

Tapping into the spiritual to understand the natural, each

piece of our life is pruned and groomed and welded into

the foundation that God ordained. Ultimately, we will see

his will manifesting our destiny before our very eyes.

It is not because we have run the fastest, were the best

prepared, or could financially afford the journey, but it is

because we stood in alignment with the creator and

persevered with determination to His plan for our lives.

> *"...So Joshua marched up from Gilgal with his entire army, including all the best fighting men. 8 The Lord said to Joshua, "Do not be afraid of them; I have given them into your hand. Not one of them will be able to withstand you. On the day the Lord gave the Amorites over to Israel, Joshua said to the Lord in the presence of Israel: "Sun, stand still over Gibeon, and you, moon, over the Valley of Aijalon." So the sun stood still, and the moon stopped, till the nation avenged itself on its enemies, as it is written in the Book of Jashar. The sun stopped in the middle of the sky and delayed going down about a full day." Joshua 10:7-13 KJV*

There may be feelings where it seems like circumstances have been held up. Not necessarily in the interest of being delayed, or denied type of thing, but more so held up. There are some hidden issues, and unspoken answers and responses needed of God, and we

must have a power to engage the spirit, to activate the throne of heaven and ask God to hold some things.

Do you ever think about, when you're trying to make an appointment and trying to get through the next green light, and you're speeding, driving and praying, "Lord just keep the light green" until I make it? Have you ever prayed, "Lord, just keep them there until I make it, or please don't let the office close until I get there"? Such is the experience of things being held up. God can hold some things in the balance. The same way that the sun and moon are suspended in the air, the stars position themselves in alignment, or the storm hides within the clouds, so is God able to halt the untimely arrival of a blessing. A blessing that our under-developed character may not be ready to receive.

It is not that he is withholding it from us or denied you of it, but it is suspended. It is suspended in the divine order and timely wisdom of God's inescapable purpose for your life. Notice the reason for the sun and moon standing still in Joshua's story. It was not because of man's power over man, but God's deliverance and glory.

When He spoke to Joshua, He foretold him that *"not one of them will be able to withstand you."* As it is written, the sun and moon did not move until the nation avenged itself. When God intends to prove a point, whether it is to you or your enemies, if heaven and earth must stand still to prove the point, then so shall it be.

Grace

God surely has a way of distracting us and reminding us that none of our problems are greater than He. In my quiet time, as I contemplate the things of this world and the circumstances of my heart, I am humbled by this reasoning. In Christ, I know and will never forget that my problems are never greater than my purpose. I am often uncomfortable and uncertain, like a ship seeking the guidance of a lighthouse, being inside of the will of God is my beacon. In all our life's aims and trajectories for success, may we never lose sight of who we are and our purpose in Christ. He arose from an earthly tomb; therefore, Christ has equipped us with an indestructible ability to push within the storms of life.

Though our sufferings be temporary, they render an eternal response of the permanent victory in Jesus through the power of prayer. He humbles us by bringing us to an insatiable hunger. Then feeds us with manna, teaching us that, *"man does not live by bread alone but by every word that comes from the mouth of the Lord."* *Deuteronomy 8:3 KJV.*

And he humbled thee, and suffered thee to hunger, and fed thee with manna, which thou knewest not, neither did thy fathers know; that he might make thee know that man doth not live by bread only, but by every word that proceedeth out of the mouth of the LORD doth man live.
Deuteronomy 8:3 KJV

Know then in your heart that as a man disciplines his son, so the Lord your God disciplines you. *"Thou shalt also consider in thine heart, that, as a man chasteneth his son, so the LORD thy God chasteneth thee." Deuteronomy 8:5 KJV.* Observe the commands of the Lord your God, walking in obedience to Him and revering Him. *"Therefore, thou shalt keep the commandments of the LORD thy God, to walk in his ways, and to fear him." Deuteronomy 8:6 KJV.* When you have eaten, and are satisfied, praise the Lord your God for the good He has given you. *"When thou hast eaten and art full, then thou shalt bless the LORD thy God for the good land which he hath given thee." Deuteronomy 8:10 KJV.*

But remember the Lord your God, for it is He who gives you the ability to produce wealth. *"But thou shalt remember the LORD thy God: for it is he that giveth thee*

power to get wealth, that he may establish his covenant

which he sware unto thy fathers, as it is this day."

Deuteronomy 8:18 KJV. You may be physically exhausted,

clinically sick, trying to fight the carnal pressures of this

world. On your knees, God is perfected, and His strength

is consuming. His bosom is refuge. His word is peace, and

His works are ever before Him.

Nothing shall withstand the power of Jesus. I pray for

you, restoration, provision, and open doors of

opportunity. Because of whom God is, we are more than

conquerors. God's grace is sufficient in all things. He

knows the very heart, depth, and intention of man. No

good thing will He withhold from you. There is a presence

in God that only faith can take you. Sometimes it is

difficult when the flesh resists and blows are rough. If you

keep seeking, not wavering, standing firm, God will surely

see you through.

Faith

I write in attempt to establish the idea of tenacious living. Prayers and hope with security, in humble obedience, assist in a forward-thinking life pattern. Life's distractions and perplexities cannot withstand a heart and mind that is established in fervent faith. Faith is defined as a complete trust or confidence in someone or something. When my way is dark, my path uncertain and I stand against the floods of this life, I press forward on the helm of the presence of God. As Hiss Spirit consumes me, the Word of God sustains me in all things, even though my spirit is vexed, and doubt attempts to weaken me.

My trust and hope are in the strength of His Word. The Lord promises that as we trust Him, holding unto the confession of our faith, *"And he shall be like a tree planted*

by the rivers of water, that bringeth forth his fruit in his

season; his leaf also shall not wither; and whatsoever he

doeth shall prosper." Psalm 1:3 KJV. It is also written: *"I*

believed; therefore, I have spoken." 2 Corinthians 4:13 KJV

Since we have that same spirit of faith, we also believe

and therefore speak and do not lose heart.

Though outwardly we are wasting away, inwardly we

are being renewed day by day. Our misfortunes and

fleeting troubles are achieving for us an eternal glory that

far outweighs them all. We fix our eyes not on what is

seen, but on what is unseen knowing that what is seen is

temporal and what is unseen is eternal. A spirit of faith is

sufficient in every trial and testing season.

Faith will charge the weary soul and cause the human

spirit to triumph. We must set our eyes, our heart, and

our tongue on Him.

We take captive the very fiber of what troubles us by the spirit of faith. No guru, medication, or vain addiction will pull you through. God's pruning work is by the spirit of faith. Hold fast, stay positive, and push through. As much as I can, I place my trust in the Lord. Even when my life is uncertain and I can find no peace, my heart is fixed on the Word. Yes, though I walk in the valley of darkness, it is written His Word is a lamp unto my feet.

Troubles attempt to distract me and circle me with fears, but it is written: "I will fear no evil, for you are with me." It is this trust that I have the courage to overcome my obstacles and simply believe. Doubt and fear flee when the promise of God upholds you. Through the grace of the cross I can boldly stand under the righteousness of Jesus.

It is by His might and will that the powers and principalities of the air have no effect against my redeemer. In Matthew it tells the story of what becomes of our faith when we forget the Word. There are times when our human nature and worldly circumstance causes us to panic and believe in fear. When we become distracted by the negatives and the blows of critical words, we lose our footing. Then, as Peter did, we fall under. But the same power that was there to save Peter is the same that can sustain us, just as Jesus spoke to Peter in Matthew 14:29, *"And he said, Come. And when Peter was come down out of the ship, he walked on the water, to go to Jesus."* When you are in a season of moving on God's word, you must continually remember the Word. Keep your eyes fixed on that which is before you.

The ability of God's power does not fade, He is still able to command the waves and the air. When it seems as though He has or has not, it should not stop you. Keep moving and keep believing, always being able to keep going in uneasy situations should make you are grip that much tighter.

Troubles of the World

Considering our numerous afflictions, cast no doubt on God. Suffer not and endure through weariness. The Master designer strategically marks your very life. Do not think that you have been forgotten to die in the desert! The navigator decided you needed some alone time with him. It is your darkest place and moment of despair that we can believe on him without question. God is present, always fit for battle and ready to act on our behalf. Too often we overlook the other set of footprints when looking at our situation. For every issue of blood, desert, valley, and night season God has already birthed a vision and activated his promised deliverance. Could I be reaching for something that is not there?

My prayer and cry to God is:

"My heart longs for your presence. Even in the turmoil, Lord, I submit myself in repentance, expressing all my faults and wrongdoing. Even when your love feels so far away and without your embrace makes me think I must be falling apart, I will keep seeking after you. As the deer pants for streams of water, so my soul pants for you, O God. As your spirit leads by the clouds, I will come running after you. As the anticipated call from a lover, how my soul longs to receive from you, how I wait for your tug in my heart, I will keep seeking after you." Sela

Reverence for the things, nature, and name of God is so important for an effectual prayer life. Often, we are so afraid of people, situations, diseases, and trials that we do not recognize the supreme nature of the God we serve.

Disrespect for God's glory and His Word reaps spiritual death. We become like Adam, trying so hard to hide in the lies of sin, that we think God can be fooled or that He does not see. Our walk with God should not be to hide sin behind his glory but receive his grace in humility and repentance. As Job says, "the Lord gave, and now he takes, shall we accept only good from God, and not troubles".

"But he said unto her, Thou speakest as one of the foolish women speaketh. What? shall we receive good at the hand of God, and shall we not receive evil? In all this did not Job sin with his lips." Job 2:10 KJV

Hang in There

No matter how we try to avoid going through the "same old, same old," we will often find ourselves plunged right back into the same situation. God allows this, but not because He intends for us to suffer or to hurt, crying in pain with tears. It is to see us grow, changing us, teaching us, and teaching us to trust him. To trust that he has a plan for us, that he is a God who will turn every difficult circumstance around.

We must take on the courage of faith and tell ourselves *Lord, I will trust you.* Trusting Him regardless of how dismal or bleak the storm looks. It may seem difficult, confusing, and oh so very self-diminishing at times; yet we must learn to trust God even still. We must take the shield of faith and praise Him for He is our provider.

As the Apostle Paul has taught us, just forget the things of the past and consider them but dung and go forward to prize of the high calling of God. When we cower in fear, give up, or lose hope, we are only giving way to the enemy to reign over us. We must remember that in all battles, be it life, love, or health, that we are triumphant. We always come out on top. God never ever allows us to settle in a pit of desperation, pity, defeat, or depression without always giving us a way out. Trial after trial, loss after loss, pain after pain.

Therefore, we should be still, and watch God prove himself. Trust the process and know that He has our best interest for us. "No GOOD thing will He withhold from me. Just because my emotions are telling me that it's difficult, that I'm feeling defeated, or it won't work, God's Word has said not so.

Hang in there, push past the hollering mouth of retreat, and know that God has me in the palm of his hand. He is bearing every burden on your behalf. Keep yourself strengthened in the light of the Lord and pull yourself together. Keep it moving forward always looking to the hills from which cometh your help. God is always there for you, and He will never leave you, nor forsake you.

No matter how far you may think that God is from your storm, He is always right there waiting. Like Peter who let fear stop His faith, God says, "come, I have this." Just step out of the boat, ignore the storm, keep your eyes fixed on Him and He will fix it. There are so many times when I have felt that way that I didn't believe in myself, not wanting to show any weakness, but you have to overcome that.

That feeling is normal, but He is more than you are feeling. You will win because the battle is in the Lord's intentional plan, and it is already won. God is a miracle maker. Truly we have heard of and have seen proof of the impossibilities, not the least of which was the resurrection of Christ! If we shall set our attention, our eyes, and hearts toward the miracles of God, then what shall I say to these things. When my situation has immobilized me, God is still yet moving. When I have set my thoughts on the things above and not beneath, or on things yet to come and not how they are, then I am surely not to give up! There is no giving up. You have been revived to run the race. *"But if I go to the east, he is not there; if I go to the west, I do not find him. When he is at work in the north, I do not see him; when he turns to the south, I catch no*

glimpse of him. But he knows the way that I take; when he

has tested me, I will come forth as gold."

Job stated, while he was yet in misery, "those who are at ease, have contempt for misfortune, as the fate of those whose feet are slipping; yet he declared, "though he slay me, yet will I hope in him...Indeed, this will turn out for my deliverance." Job 23:8-10 KJV

Perseverance

There is an insatiable feeling inside my chest that consumes my very soul. I get the abnormal urge of having something to say that I cannot put into words. Something has visited me. Something is moving in me. God is moving. In my imperfect ways, my righteousness surely is as a filthy rag. When my sins have me most unworthy, He loves me even still. When my enemies stand against me, He stands with me. When they strike out at me, He becomes my shield. When they think they have me defeated me, He whispers in my ear, "I am with you." God's love tells me that nothing shall separate me from Him, and no man can pluck me from His hands. His unfailing covers me and the power of His Word becomes the sword that vindicates me.

I am because He is, He was, and will be forever more. My struggles, though not seen by many, were all done to groom me for your ultimate plan of salvation. I came to know Him, for myself. To whom much is given, much is required; therefore, I do not take my blessings lightly because in everything I am to serve. Nothing is more effectually fervent than laying at the feet of Jesus Christ when all else has failed. Humility in Jesus comes with an understanding that you will meet various types of opposition. In our innocence, we may suffer unjustly because we are either misunderstood or not in the majority. Perseverance becomes the key to fearlessly moving forward. When all of the people and all of the things fall away, His faith will sustain you.

Life may throw you into a den of depression, doubt,

bankruptcy, or loneliness, but God covers you in peace

and brings the planned attack to its knees.

Hope

Ever felt like your dreams are bigger than your reality? This is the very moment where you decide to dig your heels in harder and get knee deep, exercising faith. Exercising your faith, the same way an athlete trains for the biggest event in their life. There are going to be failures and times when things get upside down. You are going to feel weak and like you are not fit enough to proceed. But each day, you get up in all kinds of weather, storms, and circumstance and you train anyway. You keep the vision set before you. You may not have anyone rooting for you, no one to say hang in there, but you lace up your shoes anyway.

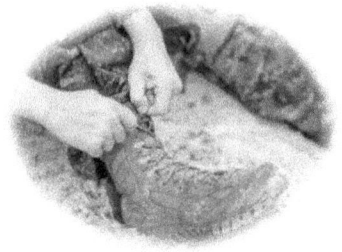

Faith is an act, and it comes by doing, trying, and working. An athlete has the ability, but talent comes from the training.

"Know ye not that they which run in a race run all, but one receiveth the prize? So run, that ye may obtain. And every man that striveth for the mastery is temperate in all things. Now they do it to obtain a corruptible crown; but we are incorruptible. I therefore so run, not as uncertainly; so fight I, not as one that beateth the air: But I keep under my body, and bring it into subjection: lest that by any means, when I have preached to others, I myself should be a castaway. 1 Corinthians 9: 24-27 KJV.

We all have the capacity to believe, but it is when we keep believing, despite of, that we develop faith. Kneel, keep your head up, and eyes forward: pray, look up to the hills

from which come your help, a. keep your eyes set on the dream at hand.

Even so faith if it hath not works, is dead, being alone. James 2:17 KJV

I will trust God. We want so badly sometimes to force the hand of God to move. Sometimes, that petition may seem as though it was ignored. Prematurely, we cause things to move. The apple always grows on the tree in its season. Fruit that is not ripe is not fit, but the ripest of fruits grows in the turmoil of the winds bringing with it the joy of life.

Forgiveness

The Lord is such a wonderful counselor. We pray for the spirit of peace and faith in forgiveness to be imparted with the family. In the time of family crisis and calamity, God is allowing moments of reconciliation, either with him or with those we love. Forgiveness is not discounting that someone has wronged or hurt us, but it is saying that I am desiring to love through compassion and see beyond fault. It is showing the same act of faith in forgiveness that Christ showed on the cross.

We ask that the love of Christ and His spirit of peace continues to mend broken hearts. God is able to restore that which is broken, and we ask that the courage of God's love meets them with what is needed.

*"Behold, it was for my peace that I had
intense bitterness; but You have loved
back my life from the pit of corruption and
nothingness, for You have cast all my sins
behind Your back." Isaiah 38:17 KJV*

In his well doing, God can restore all things. Our pain and dissatisfaction with life provides God with opportunity to prune and plan our blessings. There would be no meaning in the love of this life if we were not able to understand the presence of God's peace.

The older you get, especially if you are paying attention to what's happening around you, you see things through a different lens. It becomes less of what people may think and more of what will work for you. You should have fun while doing it.

Look at the credentials of those that judge you and don't give them any weight or power over you. Are you truly doing and being who God says you are or what others say you are? Self-reflection and forgiveness are the best medicine for burdens.

Every encounter you have with someone is never void of purpose. There is always a reason for the people you meet. It is up to you to recognize it. I live my life in, on, and with purpose. Who you are is no accident? It was purposefully thought out, well planned, and executed with loving details. Therefore, know that your very steps have been ordered by the Lord and it is well.

Poetry

Poetry is an intimate form of communication that is

becomes a visual representation of a person. My poetry

writing began as a place of retreat for dealing with what I

was going through while

growing up. I began writing

poetry in the seventh grade,

around 12 years old. My

writing became who I was and

who did always allow those

around me to see. I share a couple of pieces from earlier

writings and few pieces from later in life. The following

poems reflect me, what I was experiencing at the time

they were written, and how I was evolving.

Crying

From the depths of your emotions, is where my birth

begins,

Pulling strength from the pulsations of your heart, my life

from your pain,

As it pools in your fragile soul, awaiting my eruption,

You're trying to hold me back, to expose me in a private

place. Intense I am and incontrollable I've become,

As my presence releases from your face, drop after drop,

as I land in your hand,

I can feel you still fighting, trying to hold me in,

Fighting to regain control, but your emotions won't allow

it, And I painfully flow on.

Your body is drained, you start to feel fatigued,

Aimlessly your mind wonders in confusion, as you keep

trying,

To put the best face forward has brought you to crying.

Tears of Fear

Silence, silence, silence please

The voices in my head have brought me to my knees.

A stream of water, falling from my face,

Marks the sign of weakness, I'm falling from grace.

Slowly I cry, rethinking my past,

Dark clouds, dim lights, my time is coming at last.

It's seeping upon me like the dark van that creeps at night,

pools of black water are darkening my sight.

My crying now, I cannot control....

These tears I show, I cannot hold...

Hold back the pain that begins this battle of insanity that has surfaced here,

While alone I shed my Tears of fear.

The Mask

The person I am, changes with time...

I become a new me, to hide the feelings inside.

The new me is like a mask, through it no one can see,

Only I know what secrets I keep.

I keep my feelings trapped in, what good for telling anyone,

They'll think I'm crazy and laugh when I'm done.

Should I let it all out and free this caged soul?

Or should I keep it all in and my story untold.

My eyes are sealed, and the Mask revealed.

The real me, longing to speak,

but I'm afraid, anguished, and weak.

This mask helps me fit in, in places where I ran from,

It assures me of who I am and what I can become.

It covers the ugliness that I see in myself,

It hides the scars that pain left.

As the mask lives on, I can hear depression creeping up from behind,

Once again, I duplicate and now in my heart, two of me lies.

At this point in my life my goals come to an end,

Stress awakens and failure seeps in.

Is it too much too handle or too few to take on,

Are depression and stress here to make me strong?

My eyes are sealed, and the mask revealed,

In time I've lived and the mask as my shield.

Always the Same

My life has been full of ups and downs, twists and turns,

Some bitter disappointments, with a few laughs along the way,

In my walk with Christ, I have often become weary, not giving up but giving out...

There was a time when I thought I had lost all hope,

A fight and struggle that I was sinking in...

Tears shed because my joy never came in the morning, and a thick haze of thunderous clouds seemed to follow me wherever I would go...

Betrayed by friends, feelings of abandonment and loneliness whispering from a dark corner...

In the midst of such depravity, one thing that has remained constant and consistent, is the word of God.

Despite the uncertainty that I moved in,

the hurt that I acted out in anger,

or the flaws that I hid behind tears,

Jesus had always been the same.

...Always there to remind me to be patient, to endure, to hold on, that he'll carry me through...

...Always the same; unlike so many people you care not to name or so many "I remember when" you care not to entertain...

Although I have not had some desires received or dreams fulfilled,

I can rest in the Lord, waiting patiently, for HE shall always be the same.

Fearlessly Forward

Though I have failed so many times before, often losing confidence and my hope dimmed,

I know that I don't have to give up.

Though my track record isn't one of many good reports, and my history can't be cleared like a web browser,

I know I don't have to give up.

Though I cannot see what is before me and I don't know what the future holds,

nor what plans have been laid,

I know that I don't have to give up.

Since I have difficulties trusting, I usually doubt that anything good will come to me. Retreating and succumbing to the negative thoughts echoing inside of me.

I know I don't have to give up.

Tomorrow may never rise before my face.

My morning may never shed the light of day.

When lost in the wilderness, never knowing my way,

I know that I don't have to give up.

I know that there's a place prepared for me.

Blessings are going to overtake the tides of the sea.

My storms are the propelling force that loosens the bondage of defeat and sets me free.

When left to bleed and famished at my lowest point,

In the screams of a fainting will, faith then whispers in my ear,

"You know you don't have to give up".

Afterword

Scriptures retrieved from:

King James Bible. (2022). King James Bible Online. https://www.kingjamesbibleonline.org/

Author's Note

Dear Reader,

Thank you for buying and reading my first book. I hope you were able to draw inspiration and find encouragement from the shared stories, meditations, or poems. Thank you again for taking the time to read Conversations & Prayers.

Acknowledgment

I want to take this opportunity to first thank God for giving me the strength and the insight to write this book. To my husband from reading when I needed him to read, thank you. To Dr. George Robertson, your patience and guidance, with proofing, thank you. I have the pleasure to be a witness to your life and wife, Martha. To Martha, thank for being diligent, persistent, and you. May your family celebrate you both. To my friends who have been constant, I say thank you. May I give you your flowers while you yet live. To those extended social media family on Instagram, Facebook and TikTok. Every day I am inspired by your stories of overcoming, transitioning into the unknown and loving on yourself. Again, thank you all.

About the Author

Dr. Katoria Westbrook-Stewart is originally from Fort Lauderdale, Fl. She moved to Tallahassee, Fl in 2000, after completing high school, to attend Florida A&M University.

Dr. Stewart has 23 years of nursing experience amassing several areas of the healthcare industry. She holds a terminal degree of Doctorate in Nursing Practice with other career certifications.

Her writings have been previously shared during her formative years through school publications. She has published writings in "From the Vineyard Magazine-Miami".

She shares her relationship with Jesus to anyone she would encounters and online through her Women's Ministry: Daughters of Zion.

She is the founder of a Healthcare Educational Consulting company: Sunn Medical, LLC.

She is married to Mr. Fredric Stewart. She has one daughter, Nabrea.

Dr. Stewart can be reached via email at: proverb31n10@gmail.com.

www.ingramcontent.com/pod-product-compliance
Lightning Source LLC
Chambersburg PA
CBHW060351050426
42449CB00011B/2920